W9-BTF-445

A SHORT WALK FROM THE STATION

ALSO BY PHYLLIS McGINLEY

Stones from a Glass House
On the Contrary
One More Manhattan
Pocketful of Wry
Husbands Are Difficult

A Short Walk from the Station

by PHYLLIS McGINLEY

Illustrated by Roberta Macdonald

New York · 1951

THE VIKING PRESS

Published by The Viking Press in November 1951

Published on the same day in the Dominion of Canada
by The Macmillan Company of Canada Limited

Grateful acknowledgment is made to *The New Yorker* in which all but seven of these poems originally appeared; also to *The Atlantic, Cosmopolitan, Good Housekeeping, Mademoiselle, The Saturday Evening Post*; and to *Harper's* where "Suburbia, of Thee I Sing" first appeared.

PRINTED IN U.S.A. BY
The Haddon Craftsmen, Inc., Scranton, Pa.

CONTENTS

SUBURBIA, OF THEE I SING!

Twenty miles east of New York City as the New Haven Railroad flies sits a village I shall call Spruce Manor. The Boston Post Road, there, for the length of two blocks, becomes Main Street, and on one side of that thundering thoroughfare are the grocery stores and the drugstores and the Village Spa where teen-agers gather of an afternoon to drink their Cokes and speak their curious confidences. There one finds the shoe repairers and the dry cleaners and the secondhand stores which sell "antiques" and the stationery stores which dispense comic books to ten-year-olds and greeting cards and lending library masterpieces to their mothers. On the opposite side stand the bank, the Fire House, the Public Library. The rest of this town of perhaps four or five thousand people lies to the south and is bounded largely by Long Island Sound, curving protectively on three borders. The movie theater (dedicated to the showing of second-run, single-feature pictures) and the grade schools lie north, beyond the Post Road, and that is a source of worry to Spruce Manorites. They are always a little uneasy about the children, crossing, perhaps, before the lights are safely green. However, two excellent policemen—Mr. Crowley and Mr. Lang—station themselves at the intersections four times a day and so far there have been no accidents.

Spruce Manor in the spring and summer and fall is a pretty town, full of gardens and old elms. (There are few spruces, but the village council is considering planting a few on the station plaza, out of sheer patriotism.) In the winter the houses reveal themselves as comfortable, well kept, architecturally insignificant. Then one can see the town for what it is and has been since it left off being farm and woodland some sixty years ago—the epitome of Suburbia, not the country and certainly not the city. It is a commuter's town, the living center of a web that unrolls each morning as the men swing aboard the locals, and contracts again in the evening when they return. By day, with even the children pent in schools, it is a village of women. They trundle mobile baskets at the A & P, they sit under driers at the hairdressers, they sweep their porches and set out bulbs and stitch up slip-covers. Only on week ends does it become heterogeneous and lively, the parking places difficult to find.

Spruce Manor has no country club of its own, though devoted golfers have their choice of two or three not far away. It does have a small yacht club and a beach, which can be used by anyone who rents or owns a house here. The village supports a little park with playground equipment and a counselor, where children, unattended by parents, can spend summer days if they have no more pressing engagements.

It is a town not wholly without traditions. Residents will point out the two-hundred-year-old Manor house, now a minor museum; and in the autumn they line the streets on a scheduled evening to watch the Volunteer Firemen parade. That is a fine occasion, with so many heads of households marching in their red blouses and white gloves, some with flaming helmets, some swinging lanterns, most of them genially out of step. There is a bigger parade on Memorial Day, with more marchers than watchers and with the Catholic priest, the rabbi, and the Protestant ministers each delivering a short prayer when the paraders gather near the War Memorial. On the whole, however, outside of contributing generously to the Community Chest, Manorites are not addicted to municipal get-togethers.

No one is very poor here and not many families rich enough to be awesome. In fact, there is not much to distinguish Spruce Manor from any other of a thousand suburbs outside of New York City or San Francisco or Detroit or Chicago or even Stockholm, for that matter. Except for one thing. For some reason, Spruce Manor has become a sort of symbol to writers and reporters familiar only with its name or trivial aspects. It has become a symbol of all that is middle class in the worst sense, of settled-downness or rootlessness, according to what the writer is trying to prove; of smug and prosperous medi-

ocrity or—even, in more lurid novels, of lechery at the country club and Sunday morning hangovers.

To condemn Suburbia has long been a literary cliché, anyhow. I have yet to read a book in which the suburban life was pictured as the good life or the commuter as a sympathetic figure. He is nearly as much a stock character as the old stage Irishman: the man who "spends his life riding to and from his wife," the eternal Babbitt who knows all about Buicks and nothing about Picasso, whose sanctuary is the club locker room, whose ideas spring ready-made from the illiberal newspapers. His wife plays politics at the P. T. A. and keeps up with the Joneses. Or —if the scene is more gilded and less respectable—the commuter is the high-powered advertising executive with a station wagon and an eye for the ladies, his wife a restless baggage given to too many cocktails in the afternoon.

These clichés I challenge. I have lived in the country, I have lived in the city. I have lived in an average Middle Western small town. But for the best eleven years of my life I have lived in Suburbia and I like it.

"Compromise!" cried our friends when we came here from an expensive, inconvenient, moderately fashionable tenement in Manhattan. It was the period in our lives when everyone was moving somewhere. Farther uptown, farther downtown, across town to Sutton Place, to a half-dozen rural acres in Connecticut or New Jersey or even Vermont. But no one in our rather rarefied little group was thinking of moving to the suburbs except us. They were aghast that we could find anything appealing in the thought of a middle-class house on a middle-class street in a middle-class village full of middle-class people. That we were tired of town and hoped for children, that we couldn't afford both a city apartment and a farm, they put down as feeble excuses. To this day they cannot understand us. You see, they read the books. They even write them.

Compromise? Of course we compromise. But compromise, if not the spice of life, is its solidity. It is what makes nations great and marriages happy and Spruce Manor the pleasant place it is. As for its being middle-class, what is wrong with acknowledging one's roots? And how free we are! Free of the city's noise, of its ubiquitous doormen, of the soot on the window sill and the radio in the next apartment. We have released ourselves from the seasonal hegira to the mountains or the seashore. We have only one address, one house to keep supplied with paring knives and blankets. We are free from the snows that block the countryman's roads in winter and his electricity which always goes off in a thunderstorm. I do not insist that we are typical. There is nothing really typical about any of our friends and neighbors here, and therein lies my point. The true suburbanite needs to conform less than anyone else; much less than the gentleman farmer with his remodeled salt-box or than the determined cliff dweller with his necessity for living at the right address. In Spruce Manor all addresses are right. And since we are fairly numerous here, we need not fall back on the people nearest us for total companionship. There is not here, as in a small city away from truly urban centers, some particular family whose codes must be ours. And we could not keep up with the Joneses even if we wanted to, for we know many Joneses and they are all quite different people leading the most various lives.

The Albert Joneses spent their week ends sailing, the Bertram Joneses cultivate their delphinium, the Clarence Joneses—Clarence being a handy man with a cello—are enthusiastic about amateur chamber music. The David Joneses dote on bridge, but neither of the Ernest Joneses understands it and they prefer staying home of an evening so that Ernest Jones can carve his witty caricatures out of pieces of old fruit wood. We admire one another's gardens, applaud one another's sailing records; we are too busy to compete. So long as our clapboards are painted and our hedges decently trimmed, we have fulfilled our community obligations. We can live as anonymously as in a city or we can call half the village by their first names.

On our half-acre or three-quarters we can raise enough tomatoes for our salads and assassinate enough beetles to satisfy the gardening urge. Or we can buy our vegetables at the store and put the whole place to lawn without feeling that we are neglecting our property. We can have privacy and shade and the changing of the seasons and also the Joneses next door from whom to borrow a cup of sugar or a stepladder. Despite the novelists, the shadow of the country club rests lightly on us. Half of us wouldn't be found dead with a golf stick in our hands, and loathe Saturday dances. Few of us expect to be deliriously wealthy or world famous or divorced. What we do expect is to pay off the mortgage and send our healthy children to good colleges.

For when I refer to life here, I think, of course, of living with children. Spruce Manor without children would be a paradox. The summer waters are full of them, gamboling like dolphins. The lanes are alive with them, the yards overflow with them, they possess the tennis courts and the skating pond and the vacant lots. Their roller skates wear down the asphalt and their bicycles make necessary the twenty-five-mile speed limit. They converse interminably on the telephones and enrich the dentist and the pediatrician. Who claims that a child and a half is the American middle-class average? A nice medium Spruce Manor family runs to four or five, and we count proudly, but not with amazement, the many solid households running to six, seven, eight, nine, even twelve. Our houses here are big and not new, most of them, and there is a temptation to fill them up, let the décor fall where it may.

Besides, Spruce Manor seems designed by Providence and town planning for the happiness of children. Better designed than the city; better, I say defiantly, than the country. Country mothers must be constantly arranging and contriving for their children's leisure time. There is no neighbor child next door for playmate, no school within walking distance. The ponds are dangerous to young swimmers, the woods full of poison ivy, the romantic dirt roads unsuitable for bicycles. An extra acre or two gives a fine sense of possession to an adult; it does not compensate children for the give-and-take of our village where there is always a contemporary to help swing the skipping rope or put on the catcher's mitt. Where in the country is the Friday evening dancing class or the Saturday morning movie (approved by the P. T. A.)? It is the greatest fallacy of all time that children love the country as a year-around plan. Children would take a dusty corner of Washington Square, or a city sidewalk, even, in preference to lonely sermons in stones and books in running brooks which their contemporaries cannot share.

As for the horrors of bringing up progeny in the city, for all its museums and other cultural advantages (so perfectly within reach of suburban families if they feel strongly about it), they were summed up for me one day last winter. The harried mother of one, speaking to me on the telephone just after Christmas, sighed and said, "It's been a really wonderful time for me, as vacations go. Barbara has had an engagement with a child in our apartment house every afternoon this week. I have had to take her almost nowhere." Barbara is eleven. For six of those eleven years, I realized, her mother must have dreaded Christmas vacation, not to mention spring, as a time when Barbara had to be entertained. I thought thankfully of my own daughters whom I had scarcely seen since school closed, out with their skis and their sleds and their friends, sliding down the roped-off hill half a block away, coming in hungrily for lunch and disappearing again, hearty, amused, and safe—at least as safe as any sled-borne child can be.

Spruce Manor is not Eden, of course. Our taxes are higher than we like and there is always that 8:11 in the morning to be caught and we sometimes resent the necessity of rushing from a theater to a train on a weekday evening. But the taxes pay for our really excellent schools and for our garbage collections (so that the pails of orange peels need not stand in the halls overnight as ours did in the city) and for our water supply, which does not give out every dry summer as it frequently does in the country. As for the theaters—they are twenty miles away and we don't get to them more than twice a month. But neither, I think, do many of our friends in town. The 8:11 is rather a pleasant train, too, say the husbands; it gets them to work in thirty-four minutes and they read the papers restfully on the way.

"But the suburban mind!" cry our die-hard friends in Manhattan and Connecticut. "The suburban conversation! The monotony!" They imply that they and I must scintillate or we perish. Let me anatomize Spruce Manor, for them and for the others who envision Suburbia as a congregation of mindless housewives and amoral go-getters.

From my window, now, on a June morning, I have a view. It contains neither solitary hills nor dramatic skyscrapers. But I can see my roses in bloom, and my foxglove, and an arch of trees over the lane. I think comfortably of my friends whoses houses line this and other streets rather like it. Not one of them is, so far as I know, doing any of the things that surburban ladies are popularly supposed to be doing. One of them, I happen to know, has gone bowling for her health and figure, but she has already tidied up her house and arranged to be home before the boys return from school. Some, undoubtedly, are ferociously busy in the garden. One lady is on her way to Ellis Island, bearing comfort and gifts to a Polish boy—a seventeen-year-old stowaway who did slave labor in Germany and was liberated by a cousin of

hers during the war—who is being held for attempting to attain the land of which her cousin told him. The boy has been on the Island for three months. Twice a week she takes this tedious journey, meanwhile besieging courts and immigration authorities on his behalf. This lady has a large house, a part-time maid, and five children.

My friend around the corner is finishing her third novel. She writes daily from nine-thirty until two. After that her son comes back from school and she plunges into maternity; at six, she combs her pretty hair, refreshes her lipstick, and is charming to her doctor husband. The village dancing school is run by another neighbor, as it has been for twenty years. She has sent a number of ballerinas on to the theatrical world as well as having shepherded for many a successful season the white-gloved little boys and full-skirted little girls through their first social tasks.

Some of the ladies are no doubt painting their kitchens or a nursery; one of them is painting the portrait, on assignment, of a very distinguished personage. Some of them are nurses' aides and Red Cross workers and supporters of good causes. But all find time to be friends with their families and to meet the 5:32 five nights a week. They read something besides the newest historical novel, Braque is not unidentifiable to most of them, and their conversation is for the most part as agreeable as the tables they set. The tireless bridge players, the gossips, the women bored by their husbands live perhaps in our suburb, too. Let them. Our orbits need not cross.

And what of the husbands, industriously selling bonds or practicing law or editing magazines or looking through microscopes or managing offices in the city? Do they spend their evenings and their week ends in the gaudy bars of Fifty-second Street? Or are they the perennial householders, their lives a dreary round of taking down screens and mending drains? Well, screens they have always with them, and a man who is good around the house can spend happy hours with the plumbing even on a South Sea island. Some of them cut their own lawns and some of them try to break par and some of them sail their little boats all summer with their families for crew. Some of them are village trustees for nothing a year and some listen to symphonies and some think Milton Berle ought to be President. There is a scientist who plays wonderful bebop, and a corporation executive who has bought a big old house nearby and with his own hands is gradually tearing it apart and reshaping it nearer to his heart's desire. Some of them are passionate hedge-clippers and some read Plutarch for fun. But I do not know many—though there may be such—who either kiss their neighbors' wives behind doors or whose idea of sprightly talk is to tell you the plot of an old movie.

It is June, now, as I have said. This afternoon my daughters will come home from school with a crowd of their peers at their heels. They will eat up the cookies and drink up the ginger ale and go down for a swim at the beach if the water is warm enough, that beach which is only three blocks away and open to all Spruce Manor. They will go unattended by me, since they have been swimming since they were four, and besides there are life guards and no big waves. (Even our piece of ocean is a compromise.) Presently it will be time for us to climb into our very old Studebaker—we are not car-proud in Spruce Manor—and meet the 5:32. That evening expedition is not vitally necessary, for a bus runs straight down our principal avenue from the station to the shore, and it meets all trains. But it is an event we enjoy. There is something delightfully ritualistic about the moment when the train pulls in and the men swing off, with the less sophisticated children running squealing to meet them. The women move over from the driver's seat, surrender the keys, and receive an absent-minded kiss. It is the sort of picture that wakes John Marquand screaming from his sleep. But, deluded people that we are, we do not realize how mediocre it all seems. We will eat our undistinguished meal, probably without even a cocktail to enliven it. We will drink our coffee at the table, not carry it into the living room; if a husband changes for dinner here it is into old and spotty trousers and more comfortable shoes. The children will then go through the regular childhood routine—complain about their homework, grumble about going to bed, and finally accomplish both ordeals. Perhaps later the Gerard Joneses will drop in. We will talk a great deal of unimportant chatter and compare notes on food prices; we will also discuss the headlines and disagree. (Some of us in the Manor are Republicans, some are Democrats, a few lean lightly leftward. There are probably anti-Semites and anti-Catholics and even anti-Americans. Most of us are merely anti-antis.) We will all have one highball and the Joneses will leave early. Tomorrow and tomorrow and tomorrow the pattern will be repeated. This is Suburbia.

But I think that someday people will look back on our little intervals here, on our Spruce Manor way of life, as we now look back on the Currier and Ives kind of living, with nostalgia and respect. In a world of terrible extremes, it will stand out as the safe, important medium.

Suburbia, of thee I sing!

LANDSCAPE WITH FIGURES

ABOUT CHILDREN

By all the published facts in the case,
Children belong to the human race.

Equipped with consciousness, passions, pulse,
They even grow up and become adults.

So why's the resemblance, moral or mental,
Of children to people so coincidental?

Upright out of primordial dens,
Homo walked and was sapiens.

But rare as leviathans or auks
Is—male or female—the child who walks.

He runs, he gallops, he crawls, he pounces,
Flies, leaps, stands on his head, or bounces,

Imitates snakes or the tiger stripèd
But seldom recalls he is labeled "Biped."

Which man or woman have you set sights on
Who craves to slumber with all the lights on

Yet creeps away to a lampless nook
In order to pore on a comic book?

Why, if (according to A. Gesell)
The minds of children ring clear as a bell,

Does every question one asks a tot
Receive the similar answer—"What?"

And who ever started the baseless rumor
That any child has a sense of humor?

Children conceive of no jest that's madder
Then Daddy falling from a ten-foot ladder.

Their fancies sway like jetsam and flotsam;
One minute they're winsome, the next they're swatsome.

While sweet their visages, soft their arts are,
Cold as a mermaiden's kiss their hearts are;

They comprehend neither pity nor treason.
An hour to them is a three months' season.

So who can say—this is just between us—
That children and we are a common genus,

When the selfsame nimbus is eerily worn
By a nymph, a child, and a unicorn?

SPRING COMES TO THE SUBURBS

Now green the larch; the hedges green,
  And early jonquils go a-begging.
The thoughtful man repairs his screen,
  The child emerges from his legging.

By daylight now, commuters come
  Homeward. The grackle, unimpeded,
Forsakes his charitable crumb
  To loot the lawn that's newly seeded.

Tulips are mocked for their display
  By periwinkles' self-effacement,
And benedicts on ladders sway,
  Fetching the storm sash to the basement.

Still slumbers the lethargic bee,
  The rosebush keeps its winter tag on,
But hatless to the A & P
  The shopper rides in station wagon.

Once more Good Humor's wheedling bell
  Brings out the spendthrift in the miser,
And everywhere's the lovely smell
  Of showers and soil and fertilizer.

BALLROOM DANCING CLASS

The little girls' frocks are frilly.
  The little boys' suits are blue.
On little gold chairs
They perch in pairs
  Awaiting their Friday cue.
The little boys stamp like ponies.
  The little girls coo like doves.
 The little boys pummel their cronies
  With white, enormous gloves.
And overhead from a balcony
The twittering mothers crane to see.

Though sleek the curls
Of the little girls,
  Tossing their locks like foam,

Each little boy's tie
Has slipped awry
  And his hair forgets the comb.
He harks to the tuning fiddle
  With supercilious sneers.
His voice is cracked in the middle,
  Peculiar are his ears.
And little girls' mothers nod with poise
To distracted mothers of little boys.

Curtsying to the hostess,
  The little girls dip in line.
But hobbledehoy
Bobs each little boy,
  And a ramrod is his spine.
With little girls' charms prevailing,
  Why, as the music starts,
Are the little girls' mothers paling?
  And why do they clasp their hearts
When the hostess says with an arching glance,
"Let boys choose partners before we dance"?

Now little girls sway
Like buds in May
  And tremble upon the stalk.
But little boys wear
An arrogant air
  And they swagger when they walk.
The meagerest boy grows taller.
  The shyest one's done with doubt,
As he fingers a manful collar
  And singles his charmer out,
Or rakes the circle with narrowed eyes
To choose his suitable Friday prize.
While overhead in the balcony
The little boys' mothers smile to see
On razorless cheek and beardless chin
The Lord-of-Creation look begin.

Oh, little boys beckon, little girls bend!
And little boys' mothers condescend
(As they straighten their furs and pat their pearls)
To nod to the mothers of the little girls.

Now what's that thunder upon the stair?
It's Susan wearing her Monday Air.
She gave a slip and she gave a slide
And she climbed from her crib on the Monday side.
And the sun may shine
  Or the rain may patter,
But dreary or fine,
  It doesn't matter.
The household quivers from floor to ceiling
When Susan wakes with that Monday feeling.

Everything's spiteful, everything's horrid,
The floor jumps up and attacks her forehead.
The buildings fall that she built with blocks.
Somebody's broken the music box.
Her playthings creep
  To a distant corner.
She hates Bo-Peep
  And she loathes Jack Horner.
Pins stick into her, highchairs pinch,
And cereal's awful and so is spin'ch.
The washable lamb deserts her lap,
And who in the world thought up the Nap?

Oh, childhood's garden is weeds and stubble
On Indigo Monday, day of trouble.

But what's this light in a gloomy place?
It's Susan wearing her Wednesday face.
For the crib was cozy, the crib was wide,
And Susan got up on the Wednesday side.

Let raindrops splatter,
  Or sun hold sway.
What does it matter?
  It's a lovely day.
There's music now from the nursery shelf,
And she helps to tie up her shoes herself.

Nothing is horrid, nothing is spiteful.
She thinks her parents are *too* delightful.
The lamb says "Susan" with happy bleating.
The oilcloth elephant nods a greeting.
The camel joyfully humps his hump
And the floor desists from the tiniest bump.
The storybooks keep
  Her affections whole.
She loves Bo-Peep,
  She adores King Cole.
Carrots for lunch? Well, it's immaterial.
Spinach is splendid, and so is cereal.
Her toys reside in their proper haunts
And a Nap is exactly the thing she wants.

Oh, obdurate days, I give you warning:
Be Wednesday for Susan every morning.

I call that parent rash and wild
Who'd reason with a six-year child,
Believing little twigs are bent
By calm, considered argument.

In bandying words with progeny,
There's no percentage I can see,
And people who, imprudent, do so,
Will wonder how their troubles grew so.

Now underneath this tranquil roof
Where sounder theories have their proof,
Our life is sweet, our infants happy.
In quietude dwell Mammy and Pappy.

We've sworn a stern, parental vow
That argument we won't allow.
Brooking no juvenile excess here,
We say a simple No or Yes, here,

And then, when childish wails begin
We don't debate.
We just give in.

A MALEDICTION

ON THE PEOPLE WHO HAVE BUILT A HOUSE DIRECTLY ACROSS THE ROAD FROM OURS

Across our road there used to lie
  A little meadow, semirural,
Which seemed to a suburban eye
  View pleasanter than Alp or Ural.
Four birches grew there, leaning leeward,
And apple trees without a steward.

Day lilies lit an orange flame
  In June there. We could glimpse a steeple
And look on fields, until they came—
  This pair, these proud, presumptuous people,
With prints irrevocably blue
For a tall house to block our view.

They cut the meadow down alive,
  Cut down the leeward-leaning birches
To make the stylish cinder drive
  Where now their station wagon lurches.
Down went the lilies' yellow glory
And up their sordid second story.

Despiteful folk! With half earth's soil
  On which to rear their vile enclosure,
This single meadow must they spoil,
  The one that blest our south exposure.

But they shall rue the day they marred
The vista of an angry bard.

Confusion take their walls, their house!
  May termite dwell in porch and shutter;
In closet, moth; in pantry, mouse;
  And leaks in every copper gutter.
May they be haunted by disaster,
Including cracks in all the plaster.

Let rivers through their basement flow,
  Paint peel, pipes knock, screens fail in summer.
And may they call one fiend I know
  When, weekly, they must call a plumber.
Let tradesmen do them down in battle.
And may their midnight windows rattle.

My wrath on them across our lane
  Who laid those apples low with axes!
Come, smoking chimney, clogging drain,
  Drafts under doors, and higher taxes.
Come, swarm of wasp and plague of gnat;
Come, trouble with the thermostat;
Come, faithless eaves that buckle over;
Come, crab grass where was planted clover;
Come, dogs along their borders rooting!
And let them simply *loathe* commuting.

Perhaps that will instruct them to
Ravage a poet's favorite view!

ONE CROWDED HOUR OF GLORIOUS STRIFE

I love my daughters with a love unfailing,
I love them healthy and I love them ailing.
I love them as sheep are loved by the shepherd,
With a fiery love like a lion or a leopard.
I love them gentle or inclined to mayhem—
But I love them warmest after eight-thirty A.M.

Oh, the peace like heaven
  That wraps me around,
Say, at eight-thirty-seven,
  When they're schoolroom-bound,
With the last glove mated
  And the last scarf tied,
With the pigtail plaited,
  With the pincurl dried,
And the egg disparaged,
  And the porridge sneered at,
And last night's comics furtively peered at,
The coat apprehended
  On its ultimate hook,
And the cover mended
  On the history book!

How affection swells, how my heart leaps up
As I sip my coffee from a lonely cup!
For placid as the purling of woodland waters
Is a house divested of its morning daughters.

Sweeter than the song of the lark in the sky
Are my darlings' voices as they shriek good-by—

With the last shoe burnished
  And the last pen filled,
And the bus fare furnished
  And the radio stilled;

When I've signed the excuses
  And written the notes,
And poured fresh juices
  Down ritual throats,
And rummaged for umbrellas
  Lest the day grow damper,
And rescued homework from an upstairs hamper,
And stripped my wallet
  In the daily shakedown,
And tottered to my pallet
  For a nervous breakdown.

Oh, I love my daughters with a love that's reckless
As Cornelia's for the jewels in her fabled necklace.
But Cornelia, even, must have raised three cheers
At the front door closing on her school-bent dears.

TOAST TO A REFORMER

**AFTER HAVING DEVOTED AN AFTERNOON
TO TWO VIGOROUS LITTLE BOYS**

Despite the fact I'm simply mad
  About attending fires,
I've never claimed that Nero had
  A nature one admires.

And though I sense his point of view
  On those that peek and pry,
The deed which Bluebeard used to do
  I cannot justify.

The Borgia and the Medici
  I contemplate with pain,
Nor can accept the specious plea
  That Abel goaded Cain.

But Herod saw how after while
  This sort of thing would start . . .
And he's a gentleman whom I'll
  Defend with all my heart.

FIFTEENTH ANNIVERSARY

In garden-colored boots he goes
   Ardent around perennial borders
To spray the pink, celestial rose
   Or give a weed its marching orders.

Draining at dawn his hasty cup,
   He takes a train to urban places;
By lamplight, cheerful, figures up
   The cost of camps and dental braces.

And warm upon my shoulders lays
  Impetuous at dinner table
The mantle of familiar praise
  That's better than a coat of sable.

THE TOM-TOM

This is the day for bicycles.

Yesterday was a swimming day,
  A day for splashing head over heels,
When every child would have screamed dismay
At anything less than dolphin play.
  But today they are all on wheels.
Large and little and middle-sized,
An army of children goes mechanized.
As if for a silver medal,
Around and around they pedal.

And we saw no rockets fly,
  No messenger brought the word.
Yet lonely, lonely, the beaches lie
And the saltiest bathing suit is dry
While every child sweeps breathless by
  Like a bird, like a bird.
How did they know? What sign was sent
To herald the seashore's banishment?
Who proclaimed it the time and weather
For cycling all together?

Tomorrow, or the day after,
  The pedals will lose their power.
Solemn, and yet with laughter,
They will turn to something dafter,
  All at the selfsame hour.

All of a sudden the windy heights
Will burst into gaudy bloom of kites
With a heaven-aspiring reach
And a child attached to each.

But that hour overthrown,
  The falcon kites will be grounded.
As if a bugle had blown,
  As if a signal had sounded,
They will learn as one to be monster tall
When a madness of stilts assails them all.
Together in hot compliance,
They will walk the village like giants.

If you ask them, they are perplext.
  The calendar gives no warning.
One does not tell the next,
  Yet they wake and know in the morning
(As a swallow knows the time
  For quitting a rainy land),
When the rope should whirl to the skipping-rhyme
  Or the baseball thud in the hand,
Or the multitudinous din
Of the roller skates begin.

It is something that tom-toms say.
You cannot explain it away,
  Though reason or judgment reels.
For yesterday was a swimming day
And today is the same as yesterday,
  Yet now they are all on wheels.

Cheerios
OATS!
Cheerios
OATS!
Cheerios
OATS!
Cheerios
OATS!
Kix
Kix
Kix
Kix
Kix
Kix
Post's
Krinkles
Post's
Krinkles
WHEAT
CHEX
WHEAT
CHEX
WHEAT
CHEX
GRAPE-
NUTS
FLAKES
FRESH!
GRAPE-
NUTS
FLAKES
FRESH!
GRAPE-
NUTS
FLAKES
GRAPE-
NUTS
FLAKES
FRESH!
FREE!
WOW!

COLLECTOR'S ITEMS

Some lives are filled with sorrow and woe
And some with joys ethereal.
But the days may come and the weeks may go,
My life is filled with cereal.
My cupboards bulge and my shelves are bunchy
With morsels crispy or cracked or crunchy,
With rice things, corn things,
Barley things, wheaten—
All top-of-the-morn things
And all uneaten.
Ignored they sparkle, unheard they pop
When once they've yielded the Premium Top.

For Cheerios may be just the fare
To energize whippersnappers,
But mine consider they've had their share
As soon as they've filched the wrappers.
Breathes there a child with hopes so dim
That Kix are innocent Kix to him,
Not loot for filling
His crowded coffers
With Big New Thrilling
Premium Offers?
If such (as I fervently doubt) there be,
He is no kin to my progeny.

As a gardener lusts for a marigold,
  As a miser loves what he mises,
So dotes the heart of a nine-year-old
  On sending away for prizes.
The postman rings and the mail flies hence
With Premium Tops and fifteen cents.
The postman knocks and the gifts roll in:
Guaranteed cardboard, genuine tin,
Paper gadgets and gadgets plastic,
Things that work till you lose the elastic,
Things to molder in drawers and pockets,
Magnets, parachutes, pistols, rockets,
Weapons good for a cop's assistant,
Whistles for dogs that are nonexistent,
Toys designed
  To make mothers tremble,
That fathers find
  They have to assemble,
Things Tom Mixish or Supermanish.
How gadgets come and the box tops vanish!
Then hippity-hop
To the grocer's shop
For a brand-new brand with a Premium Top.

Oh, some lives read like an open book
  And some like a legend hoary.
But life to me, wherever I look,
  Seems one long cereal story.

LAMENT OF THE NORMAL CHILD

The school where I go is a modern school
  With numerous modern graces.
And there they cling to the modern rule
  Of "Cherish the Problem Cases!"
From nine to three
I develop Me.
  I dance when I'm feeling dancy,
Or everywhere lay on
With creaking crayon
  The colors that suit my fancy.
But when the commoner tasks are done,
  Deserted, ignored, I stand.
For the rest have complexes, everyone;
  Or a hyperactive gland.
Oh, how can I ever be reconciled
  To my hatefully normal station?
Why couldn't I be a Problem Child
  Endowed with a small fixation?
Why wasn't I trained for a Problem Child
  With an Interesting Fixation?

I dread the sound of the morning bell.
  The iron has entered my soul.
I'm a square little peg who fits too well
  In a square little normal hole.

For seven years
In Mortimer Sears
  Has the Oedipus angle flourished;
And Jessamine Gray,
She cheats at play
  Because she is undernourished.
The teachers beam on Frederick Knipe
  With scientific gratitude,
For Fred, they claim, is a perfect type
  Of the Antisocial Attitude.
And Cuthbert Jones has his temper riled
  In a way professors mention.
But I am a Perfectly Normal Child,
  So I don't get any attention.
I'm nothing at all but a Normal Child,
  So I don't get the least attention.

The others jeer as they pass my way.
  They titter without forbearance.
"He's Perfectly Normal," they shrilly say,
  "With Perfectly Normal parents."
I learn to read
With a normal speed.
  I answer when I'm commanded.
Infected antrums
Don't give me tantrums.
  I don't even write left-handed.
I build with blocks when they give me blocks.
  When it's busy hour, I labor.
And I seldom delight in landing socks
  On the ear of my little neighbor.

So here, by luckier lads reviled,
  I sit on the steps alone.
Why couldn't I be a Problem Child
  With a Case to call my own?
Why wasn't I born a Problem Child
  With a Complex of my own?

DEATH AT SUPPERTIME

Between the dark and the daylight,
When the night is beginning to lower,
Comes a pause in the day's occupation,
That is known as the Children's Hour.

Then endeth the skipping and skating,
The giggles, the tantrums, and tears,
When, the innocent voices abating,
Alert grow the innocent ears.

The little boys leap from the stairways,
  Girls lay down their dolls on the dot,
For promptly at five o'er the airways
  Comes violence geared to the tot.

Comes murder, comes arson, come G-men
  Pursuing unspeakable spies;
Come gangsters and tough-talking he-men
  With six-shooters strapped to their thighs;

Comes the corpse in the dust, comes the dictum
  "Ya' better start singin', ya' rat!"
While the torturer leers at his victim,
  The killer unleashes his gat.

With mayhem the twilight is reeling.
  Blood spatters, the tommy guns bark.
Hands reach for the sky or the ceiling
  As the dagger strikes home in the dark.

And lo! with what rapturous wonder
  The little ones hark to each tale
Of gambler shot down with his plunder
  Or outlaw abducting the mail.

Between the news and the tireless
  Commercials, while tempers turn sour,
Comes a season of horror by wireless,
  That is known as the Children's Hour.

SONG OF THE UNDERPRIVILEGED CHILD

Youngsters today need television for their morale as much as they need fresh air and sunshine for their health. . . . It is practically impossible for boys and girls to "hold their own" with friends and schoolmates unless television is available to them. . . . To have television is to be "cock o' the walk." Not to have it, well, that is unthinkable.—*Angelo Patri in an advertisement of the American Television Dealers and Manufacturers in the* New York Times.

Mother, my mouth is dimpled,
  Mother, my cheeks are pink.
There are stars in my eyes
From exercise
  And the vitamined juice I drink.
My way is a winning way, Mother,
  My manners a hundred proof,
But I'll never be Queen of the May, Mother—
  No aerial's on our roof.

We have no Console Model
  For viewing of Imogene,
No Super-Precision
Full-Room Vision
  Dual-Antennae Screen.
So playmates cry
As they pass me by
  With courtesy less than scanty,

"There goes the girl
Who doesn't know Berle
From Caesar or Jimmy Durante!"

What use to bind my hair, Mother,
Or cherish my childish brain?
I can't quote banter
By Eddie Cantor,
I never see Benny plain.
Though I'm lavish with treats
Like sodas and sweets,
Though my roller skates roll like jet,
Hark to the jeers
Of my youthful peers:
"She's got no video set!"

An outcast tot am I, Mother,
Stranger to fun or flatt'ry,
Pitied by none
Beneath the sun
Save God and Angelo Patri.
So turn the key in the lock, Mother,
While you kiss my tears away,
For I'll never be cock o' the walk, Mother,
I'll never be Queen of the May!

WHAT EVERY WOMAN KNOWS

When little boys are able
  To comprehend the flaws
In their December fable
  And part with Santa Claus,
Although I do not think they grieve,
How burningly they disbelieve!

They cannot wait, they cannot rest
For knowledge nibbling at the breast.
They cannot rest, they cannot wait
To set conniving parents straight.

Branding that comrade as a dunce
Who trusts the Saint they trusted once,
With rude guffaw and facial spasm
They publish their iconoclasm,
And find particularly shocking
The thought of hanging up a stocking.

But little girls (no blinder
  When faced by mortal fact)
Are cleverer and kinder
  And brimming full of tact.
The knowingness of little girls
Is hidden underneath their curls.

Obligingly, since parents fancy
The season's tinsel necromancy,
They take some pains to make pretense
Of duped and eager Innocence.

Agnostics born but Bernhardts bred,
They hang the stocking by the bed,
Listen for bells, and please their betters
By writing Kringle lengthy letters,
Only too well aware the fruit
Is shinier plunder, richer loot.

For little boys are rancorous
When robbed of any myth,
And spiteful and cantankerous
To all their kin and kith.
But little girls can draw conclusions
And profit from their lost illusions.

HOT

HERE COME THE CLOWNS, DIDN'T THEY?

Oh, the tinted tanbark! Oh, the tangy airs!
Oh, the snobbish camels and the plump performing bears!
Oh, the plumèd horses! Oh, all I fail to see
When Dulcy's at the Circus,
Sitting next to me.

It's high wire and light wire
  And no net beneath;
The girl is on the tight wire.
  She wears a spangled sheath.
It's clasp hands and hope, now,
  Trembling below—
Dare she skip the rope, now?
  I'll never know.
For just as she's turning
  And drums have begun,
Dulcy gets a yearning
  For a frankfurter bun.

Yoo-hoo, wiener man! Hurry with your pitch.
Dulcy has an appetite, so spread the mustard rich.
Give the man the money, dear; bid the man begone.
Now let's watch the lady—
But the next act's on.

The spot's glowing yellow,
  Weak grow the knees,

See the daring fellow
  On aerial trapeze.
The thunder of voices
  Is hushed as by sleep.
But just as he poises,
  Tense, for the leap,
Dimmed is the splendor,
  For, heading our way,
Dulcy spies the vendor
  With the ice-cream tray.

Is the diver rescued, flashing as he falls?
Can the juggler balance those thirty spinning balls?
Do the ponies samba, the tigers know their trade?

Comes a Circus crisis,
I'm buying lemonade.

I am keeping handy
Quarters to swap
For pink cotton candy
And warm bottled pop,
For souvenir turtles
Alive and unfed,
While Superman hurtles,
Ignored, overhead.
But someday, ah, someday,
With heart light as foam,
I'll hie to the Circus
Like pilgrim to Rome.
I'm going to the Circus
And I'll leave my daughter home.

COMPLAINT IN WOMRATH'S

My library lamp would burn more midnight watts
Could I come on a novel that wasn't about tots,
Could I open a book that didn't contain the essence
Of secret childhood or wistful adolescence,
Distilled (into four hundred pages, preface and all)
By an author afflicted with Style and Total Recall.

For the young, if they're kept out of sight, I've a deal of forbearance.
I realize modern babes must resent their parents,
Fall in love with their nursemaids, look on with innocent frown
While someone is murdered or playmates tactlessly drown,
And I comprehend that it's perfectly normal in kiddos
For little girls to be deadlier than Black Widows.

I understand all that. Still, I've never been wild
About viewing the world through the eyes of a sensitive child
Or even insensitive ones. Let me pulse, when I pulse,
Over gruesome adventures happening to adults.
The pangs that inferior Juliets feel as they grow up
Induce in me but a delicate yearning to throw up.

Ah, bring me a book
Where hero and heroine both wear that weathered look!

I'll settle for something historical, something post-Freudian,
Something purple or tough or suspenseful or plain cellu-
   loidian,
Something arty or artless, something even by Henry Green,
So long as it's peopled by characters over sixteen.

For the tale of a child may be teeming with local color,
But bores will be bores
And the younger they come, the duller.

PRIMARY EDUCATION

Pupils to Learn Tolerance Here Twice a Month—
Headline in the New York Herald Tribune.

By hook, by crook, by hair of head,
  By scruff of neck and seat of pants,
Our stubborn infants shall be led
  Along the paths of tolerance.

As bends the twig, thus grows the el-em;
  As twists the thread, the spool unwinds;
So, twice a month, we're bound to sell 'em
  The doctrine of Impartial Minds.

Tagged, labeled, catalogued, and graded,
  Sitting submissive in a queue,
Fortnightly they shall be persuaded
  To entertain the Larger View—

To stretch their hands across the ocean;
  To open up their childish hearts

And love their neighbor with devotion,
  As per the diagrams and charts;

To call the foreigner their brother
  (Unless by chance he should indorse
Some heretic opinion other
  Than that included in the Course).
By rote, by rule, by text and primer,
  By maps and slides and lectures read,
We'll see that Truth is set to simmer
  In every tot's intolerant head.

  Or so believes the Board of Ed.

THE VERY BENT TWIG

When I was a lass in my teens,
  On looking Biology's plan up
I learned the importance of Genes
  In shaping a mouse or a man up.
The Genes and the Chromosomes, Science contended,
Ancestrally guarded, haphazardly blended,
Determined the whole
  Of all animate creatures,
From shape of the soul
  To the tint of the features.

But now the psychologists tell us
  That Infancy settles our lots.
Are we happy or glum?
  Are we clever or slow?
It depends on the thumb
  That we sucked long ago
  When we first were susceptible tots.

Yoo-hoo, Heredity!
What's happened to Heredity?
We daren't thank Heredity
  For scholars or for scamps.
In the way that we develop
Family trees are little hel-op.
We're the products of our Nannies,
  Not our Grannies or our Gramps.

If Junior can't learn to spell "cat"
  And looks at his books on the dour side,
Don't turn to your spouse with a flat
  "Observe how he takes after *your* side."
He probably suffered a setback material
From early excesses of kisses or cereal.
Conversely, if same's
  Full of honors and merits,
How sunk are your claims
  To the wit he inherits!

Away with Lombroso and Mendel.
  Their notions are worthless, though quaint.
It's the way we were frocked,
  Or the way we were bibbed,
Cuddled, sung to, or rocked,
  Or unfeelingly cribbed
  That decides what we are or we ain't.

Yoo-hoo, Environment!
We're nuts about Environment.
  It's training for the Toidy, now,
  It's dandling on the lap
That forms the lifelong habits
Of both Kallikaks and Cabots.
(I don't know about the rabbits
  But it goes for Homo Sap.)

EPILOGUE

Still, don't you cry, Heredity, but listen at the door.
They'll have another theory by 1954.

HALLOWEEN

The night is moonstruck, the night is merry.
  Listen! It peals with a chime of words.
Twitters the town like an aviary,
  Haunted by voices stranger than birds'—
Haunted by shades abroad together,
  Shapes of childhood, mendicant ghosts,

Who claim the dark as their private weather,
  Walking the world in a giggling host.

They cast long shadows, or roly-poly.
  They tamper with doorbells. They chalk the stairs.
The night belongs to them, singly, wholly;
  Surer than Christmas this Feast is theirs.
Swarming past hedges like sparrows flocking,
  The gravel cracking beneath their feet,
Flutter the children. When they come knocking,
  Open the door to them, Trick or Treat.

Open the door to phantom and vagrant,
  Whistle them in from the wild outside,
For under the trees the leaves are fragrant,
  Over the houses the sky is wide,
And only a street lamp vaguely dapples
  Spellbound paths where the chestnut drops.
Comfort them quickly with candied apples.
  Stay them with pennies and lollypops.

Or they may forget how their beds are standing—
  Sheets turned down, and a light in the hall—
Forget the fire and the clock on the landing
  And never come back from the dark at all.
Coax them, wheedle them, call to them fonder
  Than ever you did on an evening yet,
For who knows whither a ghost may wander
  With mischief loose and the moon not set?

Treat them or trick them. But bar the door
Till the Shade is bewitched to a child once more.

ADVICE TO A TOT ABOUT TO LEARN THE ALPHABET

Consider, child, be prudent.
Rash infant, not so fast!
Oh, stay, my dimpled student,
Unlettered to the last.
Unless you leap before you look,
Your fate will be a trite one.
For first you'll learn to read a book
And then you'll want to write one.
The Pulitzers, the Guggenheims,
Will rank you with the winners.
You'll print a play, compose some rhymes,
And be reviewed in the Sunday *Times*
And get invited for your crimes
To Literary Dinners.

You'll be a Guest of Honor on a small, gold chair,
Consuming filet mignon with a literary air.
You'll grace the Speakers' Table, with authors flanked about,
For the Culture Groups will get you if you don't watch out.

Between the lions and parrots,
Behind the potted shrubs,
You'll munch on peas and carrots
And talk to Women's Clubs.
'Mid microphones and ferny fronds
You'll raise your cultured voice

So dowagers in diamonds
  Can listen and rejoice,
So folk who take their authors neat
  Can boast they lingered nigh one,
And from a paid, impartial seat
Can gaze upon you while you eat
And twitter that your book was *sweet,*
  But never, never buy one.

Oh, princes thrive on caviar, the poor on whey and curds,
And politicians, I infer, must eat their windy words.
It's crusts that feed the virtuous, it's cake that comforts sinners,
But writers live on bread and praise at Literary Dinners.

So shun this vain utensil
  Before it is too late.
Throw down the bitten pencil,
  Discard the perilous slate,
Else soon you'll start to scribble verse
  And then you'll write a tome,
And so you'll go from bad to worse
  And never dine at home.
You'll buy yourself an opera hat
  And learn to speak with unction
And end a Guest of Honor at
  A Literary Function.

You'll be a Guest of Honor on a hard, gold chair,
With your name upon the menu just below the bill of fare,
And you'll sing for your supper while the lesser authors pout,
For the Culture Clubs will get you if you don't watch out.

GOOD HUMOR MAN

Listen! It is the summer's self that ambles
  Through the green lanes with such a coaxing tongue.
Not birds or daisy fields were ever symbols
  More proper to the time than this bell rung
With casual insistence—no, not swallow
  Circling the roof or bee in hollyhock.
His is the season's voice, and children follow,
  Panting, from every doorway down the block.

So, long ago, in some such shrill procession
  Perhaps the Hamelin children gave pursuit
To one who wore a red-and-yellow fashion
  Instead of white, but made upon his flute
The selfsame promise plain to every comer:
Unending sweets, imperishable summer.

SONNETS FROM WESTCHESTER

COUNTRY CLUB SUNDAY

It is a beauteous morning, calm and free.
  The fairways sparkle. Gleam the shaven grasses.
Mirth fills the locker rooms and, hastily,
  Stewards fetch ice, fresh towels, and extra glasses.

On terraces the sandaled women freshen
  Their lipstick; gather to gossip, poised and cool;
And the shrill adolescent takes possession,
  Plunging and splashing, of the swimming pool.

It is a beauteous morn, opinion grants.
  Nothing remains of last night's Summer Formal
Save palms and streamers and the wifely glance,
  Directed with more watchfulness than normal,
At listless mate who tugs his necktie loose,
Moans, shuns the light, and gulps tomato juice.

THIS SIDE OF CALVIN

The Reverend Dr. Harcourt, folk agree,
  Nodding their heads in solid satisfaction,
Is just the man for this community.
  Tall, young, urbane, but capable of action,
He pleases where he serves. He marshals out
  The younger crowd, lacks trace of clerical unction,
Cheers the Kiwanis and the Eagle Scout,
  Is popular at every public function,

And in the pulpit eloquently speaks
  On divers matters with both wit and clarity:
Art, Education, God, the Early Greeks,
  Psychiatry, Saint Paul, true Christian charity,
Vestry repairs that shortly must begin—
All things but Sin. He seldom mentions Sin.

P. T. A. TEA PARTY

The hats are flowered or the hats are furred
  According to the season. Plump and pretty,
Madam the Chairman says a plaintive word
  About the Milk-and-Midday-Lunch Committee.
The secretary, fumbling through her papers,
  Murmurs inaudibly the bleak returns
From Tuesday's Fun Fair. Someone lights the tapers
  Set, geometric, by the coffee urns.

Now from their chalky classrooms straggle in
  The apprehensive mentors of the young,
To be impaled like beetles on a pin
  By the sharp glance, the question-darting tongue
Of vested motherhood—while daylight droops
To smile and sip and talk of Hobby Groups.

DEALER'S CHOICE

Mrs. McGregor likes her hand, regards
  The sweetening pot with pleasure. This is poker
Where stud brings never less than seven cards
  And deuces are as puissant as the joker.
The Campbells have no luck tonight and, pouting,
  Blond Mrs. Campbell borders close on tears.
Four aces lose. The host, from pantry shouting,
  Sorts out requests for ginger ales and beers.

The gentlemen grow ever so faintly ribald,
  While ladies ante out of turn and blush.
The glasses empty. All the nuts are nibbled.
  Lewellyn Hatfield shows a royal flush.
And Mrs. Campbell, teeming with emotion,
Deals forth another round of spit-in-the-ocean.

EXECUTIVE'S WIFE

Her health is good. She owns to forty-one,
  Keeps her hair bright by vegetable rinses,
Has two well-nourished children—daughter and son—
  Just now away at school. Her house, with chintzes
Expensively curtained, animates the caller.
  And she is fond of Early American glass
Stacked in an English breakfront somewhat taller
  Than her best friend's. Last year she took a class

In modern drama at the County Center.
  Twice, on Good Friday, she's heard *Parsifal* sung.
She often says she might have been a painter,
  Or maybe writer; but she married young.
She diets. And with Contract she delays
The encroaching desolation of her days.

EVENING MUSICALE

Candles. Red tulips, ninety cents the bunch.
  Two lions, Grade B. A newly tuned piano.
No cocktails, but a dubious kind of punch,
  Lukewarm and weak. A harp and a soprano.
The "Lullaby" of Brahms. Somebody's cousin
  From Forest Hills, addicted to the pun.
Two dozen gentlemen; ladies, three dozen,
  Earringed and powdered. Sandwiches at one.

The ash trays few, the ventilation meager.
  Shushes to greet the late-arriving guest
Or quell the punch-bowl group. A young man eager
  To render "Danny Deever" by request.
And sixty people trying to relax
On little rented chairs with gilded backs.

VILLAGE SPA

By scribbled names on walls, by telephone number,
  Cleft heart, bold slogan, carved in every booth,
This sanctum shall be known. This holy lumber
  Proclaims a temple dedicate to Youth.
Daily in garments lawful to their tribe,
  In moccasins and sweaters, come the Exalted
To lean on spotty counters and imbibe
  Their ritual Cokes or drink a chocolate malted.

This refuge is their own. Here the cracked voice,
  Giving the secret passwords, does not falter.
And here the monstrous deity of their choice
  Sits bellowing from his fantastic altar,
A juke-box god, enshrined and well at home,
Dreadful with neon, shuddering with chrome.

BEAUTY PARLOR

The lady in Booth Three is discontented
  With her last wave, rejects the oil shampoo
As if it were a bribe. Ammonia-scented,
  The permanent begins in Number Two.
Five thinks perhaps she'd like to take a flyer
  On something upswept. Elderly Mrs. Sloane,
From Number Seven, deafened by the dryer,
  Confides abruptly in a public tone

To Miss Estelle the history of her spleen.
  Six orders sandwiches. The pages flutter,
On aproned laps, of *Look* and *Silver Screen.*
  Seven, alarmed, subsides now to a mutter,
And Three debates the problem whether to dapple
Her nails with Schoolhouse Red or Stolen Apple.

VOLUNTEER FIREMAN

Four strident whistles means the business section,
  Two longs and a short, the Manor; three, the Park.
He knows the signals vaguely. With direction
  He can unhook a ladder in the dark,
Rescue canaries, save a mattress whole
  Or pass the cups of coffee laced with brandy.
No midnight blaze but finds him ready to roll,
  Providing he's awake and the Buick handy.

Monthly he drills. But valor has its inning
  That autumn night when by an annual route,
Helmeted, gloved, with all the torches shining,
  He marches proudly in his crimson suit—
A boy of forty who has skimmed the cream
From childhood's first and most enduring dream.

LOCAL NEWSPAPER

Headlines, a little smudged, spell out the stories
  That stir the Friday village to its roots:
TOWN COUNCIL MEETS FOR MAY, MISS BABCOCK MARRIES,
  SHORE CLUB TO BAN BIKINI BATHING SUITS.
While elsewhere thunders roll or atoms shiver
  Or ultimate tyrants into dust are hurled,
Weekly small boys on bicycles deliver
  News to our doors of this more innocent world—

A capsule universe of church bazaars
  Where even the cross-stitched aprons sell on chances,
Of brush fires, births, receptions, soda bars,
  Memorial Day parades, and high-school dances,
And (though on various brinks the planet teeters)
Of fierce disputes concerned with parking meters.

LENDING LIBRARY

Between the valentines and birthday greetings
  With comical verses, midway of the aisle,
Here is a rendezvous, a place of meetings.
  Foregathers here the lady bibliophile.
A dollar down has bought her membership
  In this sorority. For three cents daily
Per paper-jacketed volume she can dip
  Deep in Frank Yerby or Miss Temple Bailey,

Lug home the current choices of the Guild
  (Commended by the press to flourish of trumpets),
Or rent a costume piece adroitly filled
  With goings on of Restoration strumpets—
And thus, well read, join in without arrears
The literary prattle of her peers.

THE 5:32

She said, If tomorrow my world were torn in two,
Blacked out, dissolved, I think I would remember
(As if transfixed in unsurrendering amber)
This hour best of all the hours I knew:

When cars came backing into the shabby station,
Children scuffing the seats, and the women driving
With ribbons around their hair, and the trains arriving,
And the men getting off with tired but practiced motion.

Yes, I would remember my life like this, she said:
Autumn, the platform red with Virginia creeper,
And a man coming toward me, smiling, the evening paper
Under his arm, and his hat pushed back on his head;

And wood smoke lying like haze on the quiet town,
And dinner waiting, and the sun not yet gone down.

NOTES AND REFLECTIONS

REFLECTIONS ON A DARK DAY

Now and then there seems some doubt
I have much to brag about.
Cleo, serpent of the Nile,
Owned a more romantic style,
Mary upped more Scottish bonnets,
Laura won diviner sonnets,
Saint Theresa's soul was sunnier,
Austen wrote a good deal funnier,
Braver far was Molly Pitcher,
Even Hetty Green got richer.

Now and then I tell my mirror:
Isolde's lovers held her dearer,
Joan was better versed in miracle,
Sappho's poems read more lyrical,
Staël attracted people wittier,
Jenny Lind could carol prettier,
And it's plain that Helen's powers
Burnt a lot more topless towers.
Still and all, there's this I've got—
They are dead and I am not.

SUBVERSIVE REFLECTIONS

If wit engendered worthy deed
  And only the good were gay,
Bad company would seldom lead
  The innocent astray.
Toward primrose pastures few would stir
  In search of light and color
Were virtuous people merrier
  Or the naughty people duller.

REFLECTIONS ON THE DAILY MAIL

For this, for this, Herodotus, despite
Snow, rain, or gloom of night,
Or cold that chills or tiger heat that parches,
Or predatory dog, or falling arches,
Some courier undismayed
(I'm quoting rather loosely from the Grecian)
Took his appointed round and was not stayed
Until its swift completion:

That I might find delivered to my door
A catalogue, a card
Announcing shantung selling by the yard
At something-eighty-four,
A notice that on Thursday I am due
For dental prophylaxis,
Two charity appeals, one copy of *Cue*,
A bill from Saks.

THE PURIST

He sauntered through the pearly town,
  Critical, chill, aloof,
And favored Heaven with a frown
  Of casual reproof;

Observed the scrolls upon the gate,
  The moons, the rings-of-Saturn,

And doubted that they followed straight
The ancient classic pattern,

Then tasted the eternal bread
And sipped the unfailing wine.
"A vintage only fair," he said,
"Scarce the authentic Vine."

He strolled to Time's extremest rim
And stopped, and cupped his ears,
And presently there came to him
The music of the spheres.

He sighed, "They flatted once or twice,
Though pleasant enough they played."
So, for a while, through Paradise
Mirth drooped and was dismayed,

Till suddenly a little gust
(Breath of his own disdain)
Blew up and scattered him like dust
Along the starry plain.

SHORT HISTORY OF MODERN MAN

Tiptoe, the weathercock
Pursues his furious search
For pure Authority.
Upon his giddy perch
(More wavering than rock),
He postures, "Follow me!

"Here's Truth from the wind's mouth.
This is the final Weather,
Revealed for man or beast."
Then he and wind, together,
Pointing but lately south,
Whirl instantly to east.

Wind veers again. He goes,
With faith as firm as ever,
Around and 'round his route.
Feeling immensely clever,
He stretches on his toes
To tell the Absolute,

Proclaiming as he spins,
"The Truth is in the West.
Forget the old illusion."
So, at each gust, begins
His unavailing quest
That comes to no conclusion—
And comes to no conclusion.

HOSTESS

Her delicate hands among the demitasses
Flutter like birds.
She smiles, and from her smiling mouth releases
A shower of words
Shrewdly designed to set
The dust of any private tête-à-tête.

Now, having drained the ceremonial cup,
Let none expect her pardon
But every guest fanatically take up
The evening's burden,
Answer the roll of names
And spring with quick obedience to the Games.

Let every voice grow shrill, let laughter rise.
He who has fed must caper.
She prowls the drawing room with watchful eyes,
Filling the glasses, passing the slips of paper,
And desperately bent
On stirring up a scheduled merriment.

No calm must fall, however brief and narrow,
Lest to her dread,
From some small knothole of silence, some hidden burrow,
The scotched snake, Thought, should rear its venomed head.

NOTE TO MY NEIGHBOR

We might as well give up the fiction
  That we can argue any view.
For what in me is pure Conviction
  Is simple Prejudice in you.

TEXT FOR TODAY

A CHEERFUL POEM WRITTEN UPON READING IN THE "NEW YORK TIMES" THAT DR. ROBERT CUSHMAN MURPHY, OF THE MUSEUM OF NATURAL HISTORY, HAS DISCOVERED ON BERMUDA SEVERAL SPECIMENS OF THE CAHOW, A BIRD BELIEVED EXTINCT SINCE 1620

Amid the dark that rims us now,
  Beset by news we cannot cherish,
Let us consider the cahow—
  That petrel which refused to perish,
In spite of gossip it had gone
The way of auk and mastodon.

Three hundred years ago or more,
  It built its nest, it spent its slumbers,
At ease upon Bermuda's shore
  In innocent, prolific numbers,
A creature of the coral reef
Credulous, gentle, and naïf.

But then the hungry settlers came
  To find those pastures stern for plowing.
The bird was edible and tame,
  So everybody went cahowing,
Till by and by, beside the water,
There were no more cahows to slaughter.

"Alas!" cried all the scientists,
  "Alas, career so brief and checkered!"
They crossed "cahow" from off the lists
  And wrote "extinct" upon the record.
And man could boast another feat
Of rendering nature obsolete.

But all the while, with stealth and skill
  (Necessity become its motto),
The shrewd cahow was nesting still
  On lonely rock, in cave and grotto;
Invincibly, and by some plan,
Three hundred years outwitting man.

O brave cahow, so stubborn-linked
  To your own island, palmed and surfy!
I'm happy you are not extinct,
  But got espied by Dr. Murphy.
You lend me hope, you give me joy,
Whom Total Man could not destroy.

You give me joy, you lend me hope
  (At any rate, what hope is bred on);
For surely if a bird can cope
  So cunningly with Armageddon,
And, snug in unimagined dens,
  Wait out its season for returning,
Why, so can Homo sapiens
  Tomorrow when the planet's burning—

Can flee, root, cower, scrabble, strive,
And rear its progeny. And survive.
Amid our ills that seem incurable,
Cahow,* you make me feel more durable.

* The *New York Times* implies the way how
Properly to pronounce it's "Ca′-how,"
While Webster gives a choice of two:
"Ca′-how" comes following "ca-hoo′."
But Dr. Murphy's on the shelf—
Says bird will cry the name itself
At nesting time, which is not now;
Might cry "ca′-how," "ca-how′," or "c'ow."
Till winter brings the final test,
I'll say "ca-how′." It rhymes the best.

LETTER TO A POLITICAL BEDFELLOW

Admitted, sir, that all along
  (As we agreed the other night)
I have most stubbornly been wrong
  And you unalterably right—
By accident. But that's the most
Which you, complacent sir, can boast.

My credo bore the taint of youth,
  It was not molded out of terror.
In hatred you embraced the truth.
  From love I wooed the flagrant error.
It is my penance, not my pride,
To stand in public at your side.

If stand I must, as people do
  When winds of conscience prick and freshen,
Mark this: My false was partly true.
  I am not one, with your procession,
Who chanced to prove, through troubled seasons,
Right—for the wrong, familiar reasons.

HONEST CONFESSION

The things are three
  Which I discern
Less easily
  As the years turn.

Three things seem sliding
  From my sight:
The line dividing
  Wrong from right;

Whereto we hie
  From where we've been to;
The needle's eye
  A thread goes into.

THE PORTENTS

ATOMIC BOMB DISASTER REHEARSED IN MICHIGAN
—*Headline in the* New York World-Telegram

TRIAL BLACKOUT OF CITY STUDIED BY OFFICIALS
—*Headline in the* New York Times

By a cloud, by rings on the moon
Or a bough that casts no shadow,
By the snowflake falling at noon
In a shriveled meadow
Do the knowing eye and the reason
Predict the season.

So who can regard the least
Of these things with pulse untroubled?
The wind has veered to the east,
The fields are stubbled,
And the shrewd airs inform
Us of the storm.

Whose hands—not yours, not mine—
Shall hold the floods in tether?
We have seen the cloud and the sign,
But we cannot stay the weather.
Run to your house. Pull fast
Your shutters on the blast.

Though there is no safety there,
I think. Nor anywhere.

WITHOUT A CLOAK

Hate has a fashionable cut.
  It is the garment man agrees on,
Snug, colorful, the proper weight
  For comfort in an icy season.

And it is weatherproof, they say—
  Becoming, also, to the spirit.
I fetched Hate homeward yesterday,
  But there it hangs. I cannot wear it.

It is a dress that suits me ill,
  However much the mode sustains me.
At once too ample and too small,
  It trips, bewilders, and confines me.

And in my blood do fevers flow,
  Corruptive, where the fabric presses,
Till I must pluck it off as though
  It were the burning shirt of Nessus.

Proud walk the people folded warm
  In Hate. They need not pray for spring.
But threadbare do I face the storm
  Or hug my hearthstone, shivering.

MELANCHOLY REFLECTIONS AFTER A LOST ARGUMENT

I always pay the verbal score
With wit, concise, selective.
I have an apt and ample store
Of ladylike invective.

My mots, retorts, and quips of speech,
Hilarious or solemn,
Placed end to end, no doubt, would reach
To any gossip column.

But what avails the epigram,
The clever and the clear shot,
Invented chiefly when I am
The only one in earshot?

And where's the good of repartee
To quell a hostile laughter,
That tardily occurs to me
A half an hour after?

God rest you merry, gentlemen,
Who nastily have caught
The art of always striking when
The irony is hot.

THE SEVEN AGES OF A NEWSPAPER SUBSCRIBER

From infancy, from childhood's earliest caper,
He loved the daily paper.

Propped on his grubby elbows, lying prone,
He took, at first, the Comics for his own.
Then, as he altered stature and his voice,
Sports were his single choice.

For a brief time, at twenty, Thought became
A desultory flame.
So with a critic eye he would peruse
The better Book Reviews.

Behold the bridegroom, then—the dazzled suitor
Turned grim commuter,
Learning without direction
To fold his paper to the Housing Section.

Forty enlarged his waistline with his wage.
The Business Page
Engrossed his mind. He liked to ponder well
The charted rise of Steel or Tel & Tel.

Choleric, pompous, and too often vext,
The fifties claimed him next.
The Editorials, then, were what he scanned.
(Even, at times, he took his pen in hand.)

But witness how the human viewpoint varies:
Of late he reads the day's Obituaries.

NOTES ON THE PREVALENCES OF LITERARY REVIVALS

It's hard
Keeping up with the avant-garde.
There was the time that Donne
Had a place in the sun.
His *lettres* were *belles* of pure gold
And they tolled and they tolled and they tolled,
Until critics in suitable haunts
Took up Kafka (Franz).
Then everyone wanted to herald
The genius of Scott Fitzgerald.
After that, among Prominent Names,
It was utterly Henry James.

In between, of course, there was room
For a Melville boom,
For a peek at Poe, for a dollop
Of Trollope,
And currently people report on
A scrambling aboard
The elegant wagons of Wharton
And Ford Madox Ford.

Oh, it's perfectly clear
That there's change when the critics forgather.
Last year was a Hawthorne year.
Coming up—Willa Cather?

And I'm happy the great ones are thriving,
But what puzzles my head
Is the thought that they needed reviving.
I had never been told they were dead.

HOME IS THE SAILOR

LINES WRITTEN UPON HEARING THAT INMATES OF SAILORS SNUG HARBOR, AN INSTITUTION WITH AN ESTIMATED THIRTY-MILLION-DOLLAR ENDOWMENT, HAVE BEEN ASKED TO SIGN OVER TO THE CORPORATION ALL PRIVATE INCOME, INCLUDING PENSIONS, SAVINGS, AND SOCIAL SECURITY MONIES.

When sailors snug in harbor sit
  And munch the bread Endowment measures,
It is not meet, it is not fit,
  That they should yearn for grosser pleasures.

What can an old man want but sleep,
  Gossip, his pipe, the daily plateful,
And Institution rules to keep,
  And prompt advice on being grateful?

The private dollar in the purse,
  The treat that is not quite a rarity,
Could breed but discontent or worse—
  Would dull the cutting edge of Charity.

Give them the ancient's proper due:
  A bed, a bench, a wall that's sunny,
And immemorial truth to chew;
  Only the rich have need of money.

REFLECTIONS ON THE BENEFITS OF KEEPING A JOURNAL

Lives of great men point a moral:
  We should prosper in our primes
And, retiring, wreathed with laurel,
  Sell our memoirs to the *Times*.

LAMENT FOR A WAVERING VIEWPOINT

I want to be a Tory
  And with the Tories stand,
Elect and bound for glory
  With a proud, congenial band.
Or in the Leftist hallways
  I gladly would abide,
But from my youth I always
  Could see the Other Side.

How comfortable to rest with
  The safe and armored folk
Congenitally blessed with
  Opinions stout as oak!
Assured that every question
  One single answer hath,
They keep a good digestion
  And whistle in their bath.

But all my views are plastic,
  With neither form nor pride.
They stretch like new elastic
  Around the Other Side;
And I grow lean and haggard
  With searching out the taint
Of hero in the blackguard,
  Of villain in the saint.

Ah, snug lie those that slumber
  Beneath Conviction's roof.
Their floors are sturdy lumber,
  Their windows, weatherproof.
But I sleep cold forever
  And cold sleep all my kind,
Born nakedly to shiver
  In the draft from an open mind.

BLUES FOR A MELODEON

A castor's loose on the buttoned chair—
  The one upholstered in shabby coral.
I never noticed, before, that tear
  In the dining-room paper.

When did the rocker cease to rock,
  The fringe sag down on the corner sofa?
All of a sudden the Meissen clock
  Has a cherub missing.

All of a sudden the plaster chips,
  The carpet frays by the morning windows;
Careless, a rod from the curtain slips,
  And the gilt is tarnished.

This is the house that I knew by heart.
  Everything here seemed sound, immortal.
When did this delicate ruin start?
  How did the moth come?

Naked by daylight, the paint is airing
  Its rags and tatters. There's dust on the mantel.
And who is that gray-haired stranger staring
  Out of my mirror?

VIEWS FROM A TERRACE

CHANT FOR A SPRING BIRTHDAY

The temperature's in the fifties,
  The welkin's ripe to ring,
And earth and I, both hale and spry,
  Attain another spring.

The earth and I together,
  Having arrived so far,
Survey the softened weather
  And praise the calendar,

For sun that lately cowered,
  This morning shines his best;
Now all the hats are flowered,
  Now all the winds are west.

Those buds not green are fiery;
  Unzippered strides the foot;
And even Time's inquiry
  Today seems gently put

Oh, season mindful of its vow!
  Oh, blue and racing sky!
The temperature's in the fifties now.
  Not yet, thank God, am I.

NURSERY RHYME

Heigh ho,
This much I know:
What they say about men
Is largely so;
What they've told about women
From Eve to Ruth
Is sober counsel,
Is gospel truth;
Tabby and Thomas
Make dubious friends.
And that's where Wisdom
Begins and ends.

MOURNING'S AT EIGHT-THIRTY

OR, A HEADLINE A DAY KEEPS EUPHORIA AWAY

'Tis day. I waken, full of cheer,
And cast the nightmare's shackle.
Hark, hark! the sanguine lark I hear
Or possibly the grackle.

Phoebus arises. So do I;
Then, tuneful from the shower,
Descend with head and courage high
To greet the breakfast hour.

All's well with all my world. I seem
A mover and a shaper
Till from the doorstep with the cream
I fetch the morning paper—

Till I fetch in the paper and my hopes begin to bleed.
There's a famine on the Danube, there's a crisis on the Tweed,

And the foes of peace are clever,
And my bonds no good whatever,
And I wish I had never
Learned to read.

The coffee curdling in my cup
Turns bitterer than tonic,
For stocks are down and steaks are up
And planes are supersonic.

Crops fail. Trains crash. The outlook's bright
For none except the coffiner,
While empires topple left and right,
Though Leftward rather oftener,

And Russia will not come to terms,
And Sikhs are full of passion,
And each advertisement affirms
My wardrobe's out of fashion.

Oh, I see by the papers we are dying by degrees.
There's a war upon our border, there's a blight upon our trees;
And to match each Wonder Drug up
That our scientists have dug up,
They have also turned the bug up
Of a painful new disease.

At eventide the journals face
In happier directions.
They like a juicy murder case,
They dote on comic sections.

But in the morning even "Books"
Sends shudders coursing through me.
The outlook for the Drama looks
Intolerably gloomy,

And though the sun with all his heart
Is shining round my shoulder,
I notice by the weather chart
Tomorrow will be colder.

Oh, I wake in the dawning and my dreams are rosy-red,
But the papers all assure me there's destruction straight ahead.
If the present's pretty dismal,
Why, the future's quite abysmal,
And I think that I'll just
crawl
back
to
bed.

RECIPE FOR A HAPPY MARRIAGE

WITH A CURTSY TO MR. BURNS

John Anderson my jo, John,
  When we were first acquaint,
I had a fault or so, John,
  And you were less than saint.
But once we'd said a brave "I do"
  And paid the parson's fee,
I set about reforming you
  And you reforming me.

John Anderson my jo, John,
  Our years have journeyed fair;
I think, as couples go, John,
  We've made a pleasant pair.
For us, contented man and wife,
  The marriage bond endures,
Since you have changed my way of life
  And I have altered yours.

Let captious people say, John,
  There's poison in that cup.
We found a simple way, John,
  To clear each difference up.
We could not swap our virtues, John,
  So this was our design:

All your bad habits I took on,
  While you adopted mine.
Until the final lightnings strike,
  It's comfortable to know
Our faults we share and share alike,
  John Anderson my jo.

INCIDENT IN THE AFTERNOON

I heard two ladies at a play—
  A comedy considered witty.
It was a Wednesday matinée
  And they had come from Garden City.
Their frocks were rather arts-and-crafts,
And they had lunched, I learned, at Schrafft's.

Although we did not speak or bow
  Or comment even on the weather,
More intimate I know them now
  Than if we'd gone to school together.
(As you must presently divine,
Their seats were rather near to mine.)

Before the curtain rose I heard
  What each had told her spouse that morning.
I learned the history, word for word,
  Of why three cooks had given warning.
Also that neither cared a straw
For domineering sons-in-law.

I heard a bridge hand, play by play.
  I heard how all's not gold that glitters.
I heard a moral résumé
  Of half a dozen baby-sitters.
I learned beyond the slightest question
Shrimps are a trial to digestion.

The lights went down. The stage was set.
  Still, in the dusk that fans the senses,
Those ladies I had never met
  Poured out their swollen confidences.
The dialogue was smart. It stirred them
To conversation. And I heard them.

Above each stylish epigram
  Wherewith the hero mocked his rival,
They proved how nicely curried lamb
  Might justify a roast's revival,
That some best-selling author's recent
Book was lively. But indecent.

I heard a list of maladies
  Their all too solid flesh was heir to.
I heard that one, in her deep freeze,
  Could store a steer, but did not care to.
A neighbor's delicate condition
I heard of, all through intermission.

They laid their lives, like open tomes,
  Upon my lap and turned the pages.
I heard their taste in hats and homes,
  Their politics, but not their ages.
So much I heard of strange and true
Almost it reconciled me to
One fact, unseemly to recall:
I did not hear the play at all.

TRIAL AND ERROR

A lady is smarter than a gentleman, maybe.
She can sew a fine seam, she can have a baby.
She can use her intuition instead of her brain.
But she can't fold a paper on a crowded train.

TO A TALKATIVE HAIRDRESSER

Too garrulous minion, stop. Be dumb.
  Attend my curls, however tarnished,
In silence. Sir, I did not come
  For your opinion, plain or varnished.

I do not wish to hear your views.
  The time is ripe for no discussion
Of hemlines current in the news,
  Politics, weather, or the Russian.

Spare me the story (while you soap)
  Of how your molars lately acted.
This little hour—or so I hope—
  Is mine for languor undistracted.

Calm is this air-conditioned grot.
  I drowse, and there might linger in me
An unaccustomed peace, but not
  If you must babble as you pin me,

If you must feel impelled to break
  My slumber with your conversation
Concerning modes, the price of steak,
  Or where you went on your vacation.

Hush! Fetch me *Vogue* and get me to
The dryer quickly as you can, sir,
Which drones no windier than you
Or duller, nor expects an answer.

TO A LADY IN A PHONE BOOTH

Plump occupant of Number Eight,
  Outside whose door I shift my parcels
And wait and wait and wait and wait
  With aching nerves and metatarsals,
I long to comprehend the truth:
What keeps you sitting in that booth?

What compact holds you like a stone?
  Whose voice, whose summons rich with power,
Has fixed you to the telephone
  These past three-quarters of an hour?
Can this be love? Or thorns and prickles?
And where do you get all those nickels?

Say, was the roof above you sold
  By nameless landlord, cruel and craven,
Till, driven by imperious cold,
  You find this nook your only haven?
Yield me the instrument you hoard,
And I will share my bed and board.

Perhaps you choose such public place
  To do your lips and change your vesture.
You have not swooned, in any case.
  A motion, an occasional gesture,
Assures me you are safe inside.
You do not sleep. You have not died.

That paper clutched within your fist—
  I cannot quite make out the heading—
Madam, is that a formal list?
  Do you, by chance, arrange a wedding?
Or—dreadful thought I dare not speak!—
Perhaps you rent here by the week.

Well, likely I shall never know.
  My arches fall, my patience ravels.
And with these bundles I must go,
  Frustrated, forth upon my travels.
Behind the unrevealing pane
The mystery and you remain.

Yet, as I totter out of line,
  A faint suspicion waxes stronger.
Oh, could it be your feet, like mine,
  Would simply bear you up no longer?
So did you happen, unaware,
Upon this cubicle, with chair,

And did it seem in all the town
One spot where you could just sit down?

WITHOUT RESERVATION

FRAGMENTS FROM THE DIARY OF A SUMMER TOURIST IN CANADA

MOUNTAIN INTERLUDE

They might just as well
  Have been holding conventions
At every hotel
  In the Scenic Laurentians.

O GOD, O MONTREAL!

In Montreal, in Montreal,
  We saw two nuns with look seraphic.
We saw the rain incessant fall
  On us and on the tangled traffic.
We saw some interesting tombs,
  A park, full many a Gothic steeple,
An inn that boasts a thousand rooms
  (All saved for other people).

PASTORAL

At quaint, old-worldly Ste. Agathe,
We got a Room. But not a Bath.

MURRAY BAY

They had no vacancies for two
At Château Murray or the Richelieu.
So we did not stay
At Murray Bay.

ANCIENT CITY

Streets of Quebec are charming to remember—
Steep, cobbled, wearing courtyards at the back,
Called by the names of saints. (Booked till September
We found the Frontenac.)
Along the river, youth went promenading
That summer eve. We watched them from a bench,
Then ate a dinner à la carte, applauding
Each other's French.
The Clarendon regretted. We fell heir to
Some guesthouse chamber, showerless and hot.
At morning we departed, taking care to
Garder la droite.

RADDLED RHYME IN PRAISE OF POODLES

Sealyhams waddle,
  Newfoundlands cuddle,
Airedales all dawdle
  On corners to grouse.
Dachshunds know oodles
  Of reasons to huddle.
But Poodles
        Walk proud in the house.

Boxers are addled
  With love. They speak twaddle;
Guests are bestraddled,
  Kissed, pummeled, embraced.
Cockers have noodles
  Enchanting to model.
But Poodles
        Have manners and taste.

Needless and idle
  On Poodle, the paddle.
Learning's a bridle
  He's panting to wear.
Ruffed to the middle,
  He'll sit or skedaddle,
Play fiddle,
        Or waltz to an air.

Collie's a breed'll
  Guard babes in the cradle;
Springers can wheedle
  A bird from a tree.
Dobermans muddle,
Pugs scorn a puddle,
Beagles can yodel,
Though slightly off key.
Scotties win medals,
Pekinese toddle,
Chows, while a riddle,
Are tempting to coddle.
Yet, kit and caboodle,
No peer has the Poodle.
For Poodle
  Thinks highly of Me.

DISSERTATION ON FURNITURE

Furniture's rather a good idea,
  And one that was early hit on.
Bureaus I'll pin to for stuffing things into,
  And sofas are nice to sit on.
Love seats cater to amorous souls,
  A mirror's a space-enhancer,
And secretaries have pigeonholes
  For letters you ought to answer.

But I sing the bed, oh, lovely device,
Flower of Furniture, Pearl without Price!
    Wide may its praises be spread.
For rugs they expect you to walk about on,
And desks were invented to work, no doubt, on,
But beds are things you can just stretch out on.
    I sing the bed!

A stove's the delight of an epicure
  Determined that he should sup right;
Pianos are grand for the strenuous band
  Who favor a posture upright;
A table's designed for holding lamps,
  And frequently, too, to eat off;
And fireplaces scatter the dews and damps
  When janitors turn the heat off.

But I sing the bed, more precious than these,
Excellent vessel of comfort and ease
And rest that is better than bread—
Dear to the heart when the night is lowering,
Dear before dinner when tempers are souring,
Dearest of all when the morn is flowering.
I sing the bed!

Then here's to the pallet the poor man seeks,
And here's to the couch of the wealthy,
A kindly spot when the brow is hot
And kindlier, still, when healthy.
And here's to the article glorified
By Messrs. De Mille and Simmons,
Where all men's ultimate joys abide,
And probably, also, women's.

For a shelf with a book has a cultured look
And spaces for vases to go on,
And a rocking chair is beyond compare
For stubbing the midnight toe on.
But it's pleasant to write a letter in bed
And breakfast always tastes better in bed
And life seems almost inviting in bed
And books are more exciting in bed
And poems are often inspired in bed
And you hardly ever get tired in bed.

So I sing the bed, by day and by night
Luxury's pinnacle, final delight,
Shelter for spirit and head,

For being born and, of course, for dying in,
For reading and writing and multiplying in,
For nodding and napping and just for lying in,
I sing the bed.

THE OLD GARDENER'S WARNING

Between one April's jonquil buds
  And the next spring's narcissus flowers,
There used to roll imperial floods
  Of months and weeks and days and hours.

The year went slow, the year went slow.
  It idled, almost to provoke us,
From the first flying of the snow
  Until the flaunting of the crocus,

And there was time to cope with roots
  Of irises, and be their master,
Or count the roses' earliest shoots
  Before one blinked and saw the aster.

But how a garden hurries now!
  The seasons blur and run together,
Leaf scarcely anchored to the bough
  Before October cuts its tether.

No vine may pause, no blossom stay
  For our regard. While lilacs hurtle,
Heedless and headlong, into May,
  The zinnia tramples down the myrtle.

And daffodils, before our eyes,
  Are caught beneath November's sickle
As the year shrinks to the day's size
  And the great flood becomes a trickle.

Quick! Run! Forbear to dillydally.
  Glance at the sky but do not mind it.
If here's the lily of the valley,
  Can winter now be far behind it?

BALLAD OF BLUE-PLATE SPECIALS

Gone are the days when myself was young and lissom,
Gone like nickel candy bars and kings and 'possum coats.
The snows of yesteryear are gone and few there are that miss 'm.
But I lament the Dollar Table d'Hôtes.

Do you mind the Dollar Dinner?
Do you recollect the fare
That was proferred saint or sinner
Once at tables everywhere?
Not a tearoom in the city,
Scarce a tavern in the town
But would serve you something pretty
If you laid a dollar down.

I remember, I remember, how the candles used to gutter,
How the napkins made of paper from one's lap were wont to slip.
Oh, the spoonbread with the chicken! Oh, the flower-printed butter!
Oh, the curtsy when you left a quarter tip!

On the daily Dollar Dinner,
There was choice of pot. or veg.,
There was soup as a beginner,
There was pie with fluted edge.

In its season corn was cob-ish,
  And the relishes were tart.
Only captious folk or snobbish
  Ever ordered à la carte.

You may seek the ancient restaurants but little will it gain you,
  Though Musak plays as sweetly and the hostess smiles as pert.
For in lone, expensive glory stands the entree on the menu,
  And tomato juice is extra like dessert.

Though the bouillon's just as pallid,
  And as dubious the glass,
Now it's extra for the salad.
  Extra comes the demitasse.
And the cream, it runneth thinner
Than it did in days of yore
Since the darling Dollar Dinner,
The delicious Dollar Dinner,
The beparsleyed Dollar Dinner
  Stars the bill of fare no more.
(I just ate a dollar dinner
  But it cost me nearly four.)

ON EVERY FRONT

Sickened by sounds of war and pillage,
  Wearied by rumors on the air
Of stricken town and wasted village
  And death and battle everywhere,
I fled the house that horror grew in,
I fled the wireless shouting ruin,
To walk alone, a hopeful comer,
In my green garden, ripe with summer.

I leaned my head above the rose
And while I watched, her natural foes—
Beetle and slug—in barbarous fettle,
Crept to consume her, leaf and petal.
I saw the ants amid the grass
In foraging battalions pass,
Driving toward their disputed goal
For loot and *Lebensraum*. The mole,
Devious, secret, like a virus,
Bored from within upon the iris.

In captured trees had flung their tents
The caterpillar regiments.
Snails went in armor, scared and chilly,
While forward moved upon the lily
The cutthroat worm; but not for long.
Checking his desultory song,

A robin pulled the raider back
With one swift aerial attack,
But to be routed in disorder
By Tabby, pouncing from a border.

In bloody dust those armies weltered.
  Horde marched upon belligerent horde.
It was not peace my garden sheltered
  But the insatiable sword.
And watching there, I sighed. But soon,
On that same summer afternoon,
I took up arms and, stoutly met,
Slew twenty slugs with no regret.

DON'T SHAKE THE BOTTLE, SHAKE YOUR MOTHER-IN-LAW

When I was young and full of rhymes
And all my days were salady,
Almost I could enjoy the times
I caught some current malady.

Then, cheerful, knocked upon my door
  The jocular physician,
With tonics and with comfort for
  My innocent condition.
Then friends would fetch me flowers
  And nurses rub my back,
And I could talk for hours
  Concerning my attack.
But now, when vapors dog me,
  What solace do I find?
My cronies can't endure me.
The doctors scorn to cure me,
And, though I ail, assure me
  It's all a state of mind.

It's psychosomatic, now, psychosomatic.
Whatever you suffer is psychosomatic.
Your liver's a-quiver? You're feeling infirm?
Dispose of the notion you harbor a germ.
Angina,
  Arthritis,
    Abdominal pain—
They're nothing but symptoms of marital strain.
They're nothing but proof that your love life is
  minus.
The ego is aching
Instead of the sinus.
So face up and brace up and stifle that sneeze.
It's psychosomatic. And ten dollars, please.

There was a time that I recall,
  If one grew pale or thinnish,

The pundits loved to lay it all
  On foods unvitaminish,
Or else, dogmatic, would maintain
  Infection somewhere acted.
And when they'd shorn the tonsils twain,
  They pulled the tooth impacted.
But now that orgies dental
  Have made a modish halt,
Your ills today are mental
  And likely all your fault.
Now specialists inform you,
  While knitting of their brows,
Your pain, though sharp and shooting,
Is caused, beyond disputing,
Because you hate commuting
  Or can't abide your spouse.

It's psychosomatic, now, psychosomatic.
You fell down the stairway? It's psychosomatic.
That sprain of the ankle while waxing the floors—
You did it on purpose to get out of chores.
Nephritis,
  Neuritis,
    A case of the ague?
You're just giving in to frustrations that plague you.
You long to be coddled, beloved, acclaimed,
So you caught the sniffles.
And aren't you ashamed!
And maybe they're right. But I sob through my wheezes,
"They've taken the fun out of having diseases."

THE CONCERT

When leaves of April glisten,
  When sunlight gilds the air,
Oh, pause a space and listen
  To music everywhere—
To aria, ballad, trio,
  Cantata, what you will,
Sung *tosto* or *con brio*
  With immemorial skill.
From lyric grasses springing,
  Green buds, melodious roots,
There comes a sound of singing
  More delicate than flutes.
And he is poor of spirit
  Or deafer than the clay
Who will not stop to hear it
  On any April day.

POEM IN PRAISE OF THE CONTINENTAL CONGRESS

A FOURTH OF JULY HYMN

Thank you, Mr. Jefferson,
  For bearding the British brass.
And thank you, Mr. Adams,
  Of Braintree (Quincy), Mass.
Carroll and Clark and Clymer,
  Harrison, Hancock, Hart,
Printer Franklin and Planter Hall,
I thank you one and I thank you all
For rising up at your country's call
  And giving the Fourth a start.
Thanks with gratitude more than cursory
For handing July an anniversary.

What is so rare in these sovereign states
As festive weather on festive dates?
Sneezes hamper the Yuletide kiss.
Autumn glooms on the Armistice.
Easter's certain to be contrary.
Washington picked out February.
But east and west and south and north
There's strawberry shortcake on the Fourth.

So hip and hip and a loud hooray
For glorious Independence Day,

Day auspicious for every comer
Because it falls on the Fourth of summer,
When winds are soft and the air's a prism
And climate's conducive to patriotism.
Fathers, I'm grateful when I remember
You might have fixed on the Fourth of November.

You might have chosen August,
  When lawns begin to parch,
Defended Man in the middle of Jan.
  Or the horrible first of March.
But you thought of parades and picnics,
  Of a blue American sky,
Of driving fast in a brand-new car,
Of rowing boats and of breaking par,
And you set it down on your calendar
  That you'd choose the Fourth of July.

So thank you, Button Gwinnett,
  For a celebration blithe.
And thank you, Roger Sherman,
  And thank you, Mr. Wythe.
Hopkinson, Hooper, Heyward,
  Livingston, Lewis, Lee,
Merchant Morris, of Morrisania,
Morton, the jurist from Pennsylvania,
I'm happy you surged with that freedomania.
  Thanks for the Land of the Free,
For giving us liberty's deathless chime
And a holiday in the summertime.

SONG FROM NEW ROCHELLE

Monday's child is fair of face,
  And her driver's a handsome fellow.
Tuesday's child is full of grace,
  So she gracefully hails a Yellow.
Wednesday's child has a red coupé,
  With a little black horn she toots.
But I was born on a Saturday,
  And Saturday's child commutes!

CHORUS

No responsibility is assumed for errors in timetables
Nor for inconvenience or damage resulting from delayed trains
Or failure to make connections.

They that live on Washington Square
  May sleep as long as they please.
And they slumber deep and they slumber fair
  In the affluent Seventies.
In Tudor City the good and mild
  Lie late with a brow serene.
But I am only Saturday's child
  So I get the eight-sixteen.

CHORUS

Buy tickets before boarding trains, and avoid
Payment of extra charge.

The other girls go out to play
  In the fields of corn and clover.
And the other girls can always stay
  Until the party's over.
But just when the height is at its fun
  And the yodeler's growing vocal,
I am the one who needs must run
  To catch the Stamford local.
It's I whom hostesses yearn to shelve;
  The Bridge-Table Blight am I.
(If Cinderella went home at twelve,
  She probably lived in Rye.)
Before the chorus has ceased to smile
  Or the maestro dropped his baton,
I am the lass in the middle aisle
  Who's trying to get her hat on.

Oh, gaiety dwells
In the best hotels,
  But little to me it boots.
For I was born
On Saturday morn
  And Saturday's child commutes.

CHORUS

The schedules shown herein are subject
To change without notice.

SONG OF CELEBRATION

FOR THE ANNUAL TERMINATION OF DAYLIGHT SAVING

Arrives the month that's meant for mine.
  Arrives my heart's entreaty.
This season is my Valentine,
  September is my sweetie.
Now worth the candle seems the game,
  The battle worth the warring,
Since what I lost when April came
  Next week they'll be restoring—
That hour the gov.
Deprived me of,
  This Sunday they're restoring.

Delightful blessing, golden boon!
  How like a gift from Heaven
To wake upon a Sabbath noon
  And find it's still eleven;
To shut the eye a second more,
  Then greet the day and thrive in it
That names its hours twenty-four
  But serves us twenty-five in it;

To slow the clock's exacting chime
  Without a sense of onus,
As if myself had wrung from Time
  This uncontested bonus—

Dine late, go late on Sunday call,
  Drink coffee late (and stronger),
And put off bed and Nembutal
  Full sixty minutes longer!

Let him who dotes on daffodil
  With admiration drunken
Lament the laboring months until
  His sleep once more is shrunken.
I praise the time when few birds sing
  And leaf's a crimson warning,
For what they filched from me last spring
  Returns on Sunday morning.
Come fires and frost!
One hour I lost
  Returns on Sunday morning.

LETTER FROM A COUNTRY INN

Dinner's at one. They ring an outside gong
To summon cottagers from down the hill.
The blue, anonymous days are seasons long,
And nights derisive with a whippoorwill.

We brag on postal cards about the blankets
We sleep beneath, or praise the altitude.
The meadow wears its butterflies like trinkets,
Gaudy and inexhaustibly renewed.

And all the hours are loud with children falling
From habitable trees or in the lake,
Forever at the tops of voices calling
The gossip that consumes them while they wake,

Pursuing goose or fleeing jealous gander,
Fishing for minnow fabulous as whale,
Or scooping up the luckless salamander
From violated pool to secret pail.

Here time swings idly as a toy balloon,
Empty of struggle, almost of thought itself.
Yesterday's paper comes this afternoon
And lies unopened on the mantel shelf,

And all is innocent and desultory
  As we'd forgotten that a world might seem.
Only at week's end does the tempo vary.
  Then dreaming women rouse themselves from dream,

Tie ribbons in their hair with rapt attention,
  Discard their knitting, put their novels down,
And half-delighted, half with apprehension,
  Await the train that carries up from town

Their stranger husbands, fetching even here
Reality's outrageous atmosphere.

DEPARTURE FROM VERMONT

Close the last cupboard, roll the rug,
  Sweep clean the hearth of ash and splinter,
Batten the final window snug
  Against imagined shapes of winter.

The station wagon at the door
  Already pants for homeways hilly.
This is farewell. One summer more
  Has withered like the Turk's-cap lily.

Now mist and pallor overtake
  The meadows where we liked to forage;
No swimmer cleaves the metal lake;
  Sailless, the sailboat sulks in storage.

Already cold the morning airs.
  At night the bullfrog counsels danger.
And this familiar landscape wears
  The sudden aspect of a stranger.

There lies a menace in the north.
  The swallows from their eaves have stolen.
So fetch the bursting luggage forth—
  Since June, miraculously swollen.

Discarding hammock to the moth,
The picnic place to brush and boulder,
Now drape the unaccustomed cloth
Of town upon the sunburnt shoulder.

This is farewell. Quick, turn the key
Upon the cricket's parting sentence
And, newly waked from languor, flee
The season's husk without repentance.

OPEN LETTER TO SANTA CLAUS

Dear Kringle or Whomever This Concerns:

Before a yule log burns
Or the first fir tree teeters on its stand,
I take my pen in hand
(Take, anyhow, a pencil in my fist)
And write this little list
Of festal boons, ingenious but sterile,
You bring me at your peril.
Here is fair warning
Of what I do not want on Christmas morning.

For instance, lamps. Fetch me no lamps of pottery,
No lamps beloved of gift shops and of brides,
No tasseled lamps from rummage sale or lottery,
None planted with ivy sprouting at the sides,
Or fashioned out of canister or churn
Discarded (rightly) by one's Grams and Gramps,
No lamps Chinese or period or Moderne.
No lamps.

Also, I would prefer
No bath towels coyly lettered "HIM" and "HER";
No matches, monogrammed; no cocktail glasses
(Planned for the rumpus rooms of those who've got'm)
With naughty silhouettes of Gallic lasses
Painted upon the bottom;

No dubious napery
Personalized and papery;
No hand-blocked scarves designed to wrap the head
  in;
No bedroom slippers
That fools as well as angels fear to tread in;
No gloves with zippers.

Likewise, I beg you, curb
Your passion for the culinary herb,
Which, though no doubt divine to flavor stew with,
I don't know what to do with.

Avoid the bath salts and the cloisonné;
The diary refillable as to leaf;
The ash—or any other kind of—tray;
The colored handkerchief;
The deck of cards with pictures of Mount Shasta on;
The pad to score Canasta on.
(In fact, best star this item with an asterisk:
I am a bad Canasta risk.)
Ah, call it treason,
But spare me, sir, such horrors of the season.
My wants are easy, small, and quickly spoken.
Leave for me
As seal of faith, as merely holiday token,
Some minor bauble underneath the tree:
Perhaps a gilt-edged bond,
Some modest pearl or simple diamond,
Or—let me think—
Something as casual as a basic mink

To shelter me from winter's chills and damps
When blizzards threaten and the blood runs thinly.

But, sir, no lamps!

Yours faithfully,

PHYLLIS MCGINLEY

PRIMAVERA

Who cares if the breeze is cold
  Or rain on the roof is drumming?
I know that buds will unfold,
  The bluebird is coming, coming.
Though weather is far from grand out,
  Hope soars on a rushing wing;
Committees are starting to hand out
  The prizes that bloom in the spring.

For better to mark
The season's arc
  Than daffodils set in rows
Is a Pulitzer Prize
Or a Bollingen Prize
Or a New York University Literature Prize
  Or the prize from Harper & Bros.

Already a rumor spreads.
  Already, in sheltered places,
The Scholarships rear their heads,
  The Medals lift up their faces.
Honors with airs arboreal
  Stream from the Catholic Press
And the Sidney Howard Memorial
  Scatters a green largess.

Oh, my spirit flames
When they're naming names
(Though it's probably simply mad o' me)
For the Critics' Award
And the Hopwood Award
And the Edith Anisfield-Wolf Award
And the ones from the National Academy.

Forget the forget-me-not,
Ignore the wind and the shower,
For look how the Caldecott
Already has burst in flower.
Let dramatists' dreams grow rosy,
Let novelists wake and sing,
And maybe they'll garner a posy
From garlands that grow in the spring.

For surer sign
Than the columbine
And more of a vernal tip
Is a Newberry Prize
Or a Red Badge Prize
Or a Herald Tribune Children's Spring Book Festival Prize
Or a Guggenheim Fellowship.

REACTIONARY ESSAY ON APPLIED SCIENCE

I cannot love the Brothers Wright.
  Marconi wins my mixed devotion.
Had no one yet discovered Flight
  Or set the air waves in commotion,
Life would, I think, have been as well.
That also goes for A. G. Bell.

What I'm really thankful for, when I'm cleaning up after lunch,
Is the invention of waxed paper.

That Edison improved my lot,
  I sometimes doubt; nor care a jitney
Whether the kettle steamed, or Watt,
  Or if the gin invented Whitney.
Better the world, I often feel,
Had nobody contrived the wheel.

On the other hand, I'm awfully indebted
To whoever it was dreamed up the elastic band.

Yes, pausing grateful, now and then,
  Upon my prim, domestic courses,
I offer praise to lesser men—
  Fultons unsung, anonymous Morses—
Whose deft and innocent devices
Pleasure my house with sweets and spices.

I give you, for instance, the fellows
Who first had the idea for Scotch Tape.

I hail the man who thought of soap,
The chap responsible for zippers,
Sun lotion, the stamped envelope,
And screens, and wading pools for nippers,
Venetian blinds of various classes,
And bobby pins and tinted glasses.

DeForest never thought up anything
So useful as a bobby pin.

Those baubles are the ones that keep
Their places, and beget no trouble,
Incite no battles, stab no sleep,
Reduce no villages to rubble,
Being primarily designed
By men of unambitious mind.

You remember how Orville Wright said his flying machine
Was going to outlaw war?

Let them on Archimedes dote
Who like to hear the planet rattling.
I cannot cast a hearty vote
For Galileo or for Gatling,
Preferring, of the Freaks of science,
The pygmies rather than the giants—

(And from experience being wary of
Greek geniuses bearing gifts)—

Deciding, on reflection calm,
  Mankind is better off with trifles:
With Band-Aid rather than the bomb,
  With safety match than safety rifles.
Let the earth fall or the earth spin!
A brave new world might well begin
With no invention
Worth the mention
Save paper towels and aspirin.

Remind me to call the repairman
About my big, new, automatically defrosting refrigerator with the built-in electric eye.

ODE TO THE END OF SUMMER

Summer, adieu.
Adieu, gregarious season.
Good-by, 'revoir, farewell.
Now day comes late; now chillier blows the breeze on
Forsaken beach and boarded-up hotel.
Now wild geese fly together in thin lines
And Tourist Homes take down their lettered signs.

It fades—this green, this lavish interval,
This time of flowers and fruits,
Of melon ripe along the orchard wall,
Of sun and sails and wrinkled linen suits;
Time when the world seems rather plus than minus
And pollen tickles the allergic sinus.

Now fugitives to farm and shore and highland
Cancel their brief escape.
The Ferris wheel is quiet at Coney Island
And quaintness trades no longer on the Cape;
While meek-eyed parents hasten down the ramps
To greet their offspring, terrible from camps.

Turn up the steam. The year is growing older.
The maple boughs are red.
Summer, farewell. Farewell the sunburnt shoulder,
Farewell the peasant kerchief on the head.
Farewell the thunderstorm, complete with lightning,
And the white shoe that ever needeth whitening.

Farewell, vacation friendships, sweet but tenuous.
Ditto to slacks and shorts.
Farewell, O strange compulsion to be strenuous
Which sends us forth to death on tennis courts.
Farewell, Mosquito, horror of our nights;
Clambakes, iced tea, and transatlantic flights.

The zinnia withers, mortal as the tulip.
Now from the dripping glass
I'll sip no more the amateur mint julep
Nor dine al fresco on the alien grass;
Nor scale the height nor breast the truculent billow
Nor lay my head on any weekend pillow.

Unstintingly I yield myself to Autumn
And Equinoctial sloth.
I hide my swim suit in the bureau's bottom
Nor fear the fury of the after-moth.
Forswearing porch and pool and beetled garden,
My heart shall rest, my arteries shall harden.

Welcome, kind Fall, and every month with "r" in
Whereto my mind is bent.
Come, sedentary season that I star in,
O fire-lit Winter of my deep content!
Amid the snow, the sleet, the blizzard's raw gust,
I shall be cozier than I was in August.

Safe from the picnic sleeps the unlittered dell.
The last Good Humor sounds its final bell,
And all is silence.
Summer, farewell, farewell.

I KNOW A VILLAGE

I know a village facing toward
  Water less sullen than the sea's,
Where flickers get their bed and board
  And all the streets are named for trees.

The streets are named for trees. They edge
  Past random houses, safely fenced
With paling or with privet hedge
  That bicycles can lean against.

And when the roots of maples heave
  The solid pavements up that bound them,
Strollers on sidewalks give them leave
  To thrust, and pick a way around them.

The little boats in harbor wear
  Sails whiter than a summer wedding.
One fountain splashes in a Square.
  In winter there's a hill for sledding;

While through October afternoons
  Horse chestnuts dribble on the grass,
Prized above diamonds or doubloons
  By miser children, shrill from class.

I know a village full of bees
  And gardens lit by canna torches,
Where all the streets are named for trees
  And people visit on their porches.

It looks haphazard to the shore.
  Brown flickers build there. And I'd not
Willing, I think, exchange it for
  Arcadia or Camelot.